Luann Dunnuck

Chocolate, Peanut Butter & Life

CREATION
HOUSE
A STRANG COMPANY

CHOCOLATE, PEANUT BUTTER, AND LIFE
by Luann Dunnuck
Published by Creation House
A Strang Company
600 Rinehart Road
Lake Mary, Florida 32746
www.creationhouse.com

Cover design by Amanda Potter

Library of Congress Control Number: 2008923859
International Standard Book Number: 978-1-59979-353-5

First Edition

08 09 10 11 12 — 9 8 7 6 5 4 3 2 1
Printed in the United States of America

Dedication

To my two daughters, Gabrielle and Sophia: I have had so much fun baking with you, and of course, eating the spoils of our culinary concoctions.

To my husband: where would I be without your strength and support? Thank you for believing in my dreams.

To all the wonderful Italian cooks in my family: you have inspired me more than you know!

Contents

Introduction

I HAVE HAD A propensity toward peanut butter cups for over twenty years. I remember being ten years old and collecting Reese's Peanut Butter Cups wrappers in my top dresser drawer. The Hershey Company was offering some sort of prize that I thought surely I would win, given all of the peanut butter cups that I ate.

Peanut butter cups always remind me that no matter what you're going through or what you've already been through, there is always a small gift of simplicity for you to enjoy. I decided to combine my love of chocolate and peanut butter with my desire to motivate and cheer others on. Hence, *Chocolate, Peanut Butter, and Life* was created.

Many times we take life too seriously. We have schedules to follow, to do lists to accomplish, and chores to complete. But there is a lighter side to your existence. Sometimes we need to enjoy the simple side of life, the side that includes dessert. In this book you will find something sweet for the body and soul. You will find encouraging excerpts that will put a smile on your face and a bounce in your step. The recipes I've included—a collection of my favorite desserts— are not only delicious but easy to prepare.

As much as I enjoy practicing exercise and healthy eating, I will splurge on a good dessert. Eating well is important; in fact, it's the key to maintaining good health. But occasionally I like to make a special dessert for my family to enjoy. So to those of you who like to bake, go ahead and create something to share with your family and friends.

Speaking of putting things together, you and I have been put together very carefully and with much creativity. We have been designed to live life to the fullest, but do we live our lives this way? It is my hope that after reading the motivating selections found in this book you will be invigorated and inspired to live your life to the maximum potential.

1

The Peanut Butter Cup
That Wishes It Were
a Snickers Bar

THE PEANUT BUTTER cup is proof that there is a God. Only God in His wisdom could have given man the idea to combine rich chocolate with creamy peanut butter. The end result is culinary splendor. God made you with the same creative genius, but perhaps you've found accepting the way you were designed to be a challenge at times.

It's important to accept who you are. You will never be like your friend or the person on TV, but you have been blessed with being you. Accepting your gifts and talents will enable you to walk in confidence. Once you let go of inferiority and learn to be happy being you, a peace will begin to envelop your life. Make the decision today to accept yourself just the way you are. You are growing and changing into the person God has destined you to become.

Remember, you are far more valuable than the peanut butter cup. You are created with a purpose and a plan in mind. Lift up your head and know that God has endowed you with good qualities. He has given you talents and gifts not to be hidden or kept in the dark, but to be used to bring good into the world.

If God has created you to be a peanut butter cup, don't

envy the Snickers bar. If God has created you an M&M, don't envy the 3 Musketeers. You are created beautifully, and there is a purpose in your design!

 This recipe came out of attempting to throw something together one night to bring to a friend's house. I got the notion that if people add chocolate chips to brownies, why not smother the top of the brownies with chocolate chips and peanut butter chips? My quick idea ended up being one of my favorite chocolate-peanut butter dishes.

Chocolate-Peanut Butter Brownies

1 box brownie mix
12 oz. semi-sweet chocolate chips
12 oz. peanut butter chips

Prepare the brownies according to package directions, being careful not to overbake. As soon as the brownies come out of the oven, pour the package of peanut butter chips over the hot brownies. Then pour the desired quantity of chocolate chips over the brownies, depending on how much chocolate you like. The peanut butter chips and chocolate chips will melt from the heat of the brownies.

Allow the brownies to cool, then cut them in squares and serve.

2

The Faithful Baker

G OD WOULD MOVE heaven and Earth to help you. I challenge you to look back in your life and see how God has been faithful to you, to carefully remember how He turned impossibilities into realities and how He continues to help, provide, or in some way show His kindness to you. God says that He looks for someone to bless and show favor.

For the eyes of the LORD run to and fro throughout the whole earth, to show Himself strong on behalf of those whose heart is loyal to Him.

—2 Chronicles 16:9

Catch what God is saying: He wants to show Himself strong to you. This is a characteristic of God, and this is how He longs to reveal Himself to you. The God that set the stars, moon, and sun in place actually looks for someone to bless.

It's not about being perfect. It's about being surrendered. I know in times past I have misjudged God, thinking that He was a hard taskmaster. The opposite is true. He is a loving God that longs to be good to us. I once talked to a woman who thought God and the devil were one deity. After several minutes of trying to explain to her that this was simply not true, I walked away from her shaking my head, thinking to myself that she had a screw loose. A few minutes later a thought popped into my head: "Isn't that what you believe?" I stopped in my tracks. The thought continued, "You believe I'm a loving God, but you also believe I am cruel enough to leave you in your pain." I repented at that moment, and I have never again accused God of being cruel to me or of not helping.

Distinguish today between the characteristics of a loving God and the cruelty of the enemy of our soul. Know that God only has your best interest in mind.

This dessert was a light bulb moment. Why not bake chocolate cupcakes and add miniature peanut butter cups to the cupcakes? A true chocolate-peanut butter cup lover finds many ways to incorporate peanut butter cups into just about anything. Enjoy this simple dessert!

Chocolate-Peanut Butter Cupcakes

1 box chocolate cake mix
60 miniature peanut butter cups
1 can chocolate frosting or 2 cups of your favorite homemade chocolate frosting recipe (I use the one on the back of the Hershey cocoa box.)

Prepare the chocolate cake mix according to package directions for cupcakes.

Take the cupcakes out of the oven during the last 10 minutes of their baking time and put 2 miniature peanut butter cups into each hot cupcake. Put the cupcakes back in the oven for their remaining 10 minutes.

After removing the cupcakes from the oven, let them cool to room temperature before frosting them with your favorite chocolate frosting.

TIP You may want to substitute vanilla cake mix in place of chocolate if the recipe is too rich for your taste.

3

Don't Condemn the Chocolate

*H*AVE YOU EVER put yourself down for something you said or did? Have you ever spent countless hours or even days replaying your actions or words? This is called self-condemnation. According to Webster's dictionary, *condemnation* means "to pronounce wrong, to blame and to utterly reject."[1] Do you realize, every time we condemn ourselves we are, in essence, rejecting ourselves? Speaking as someone who has had much practice in this area, this becomes exhausting! I have come to a place in my life where I don't want to waste any more time putting myself down, and neither should you.

I encourage you to become mindful of your inner dialogue. Are you speaking to yourself in a way that is counterproductive to living a successful life? Only you can make the decision to like who you are despite your weakness and flaws. When we acknowledge our mistakes and make any wrongs right, then it's time to let go. It's time to stop blaming ourselves and choose to free ourselves from any self-hate.

The most familiar scripture concerning condemnation is found in the book of Romans.

> *There is therefore now no condemnation to them which
> are in Christ Jesus, who walk not after the flesh, but
> after the Spirit.*
>
> —Romans 8:1, KJV

We learn in this passage that we are no longer slaves to condemnation. One commentary said, "Paul's statement of lifting this blame off of us, brings peace of mind."[2] We are filled with peace when we choose to not walk in condemnation.

Jesus took all our sin, guilt, and condemnation on the cross. He died so that we could be free. A friend once told me, "You've been existing. It's time to start living!" This statement is filled with an insightful truth. We spend too much time on the negative in our lives and not enough time on living life with purpose. You see, the Cross is available to release us from condemnation and from any past mistakes. Are we going to fail in this life? Yes. Do we have to stay stuck in our mistakes? Absolutely not! God's will is that we don't blame ourselves for days, months, or even years. Pick yourself up, hold your head up high, and know that you are doing the best that you can. You can choose to be free from guilt and condemnation.

This recipe was created during one of those hot summer months when you just want to eat ice cream for breakfast, lunch, and dinner. I got the notion of using a chocolate piecrust—you always know whatever else you add to a chocolate piecrust is going to be good—and, of course, peanut butter cups. How could you go wrong with ice cream, peanut butter cups, chocolate syrup, and a chocolate piecrust? This definitely satisfies the ice cream craving. By the way, don't rule this out for the winter months. I like eating my ice cream in the winter in front of a fireplace.

Chocolate-Peanut Butter Ice Cream Pie

1 pre-baked chocolate piecrust (such as Keebler Ready-Crust brand in the baking aisle)
3½ c. premium vanilla ice cream, softened slightly
12 peanut butter cups, quartered
8 oz. whipped topping
2 Tbsp. chocolate syrup

Cover the bottom of the chocolate crust with half of the peanut butter cup pieces. Drizzle 1 tablespoon of chocolate syrup over peanut butter cups. Next, fill the pie with vanilla ice cream. Top the ice cream layer with the leftover peanut butter cups, reserving 4 candy wedges for a garnish at the end. Sprinkle remaining chocolate syrup over the top of the pie. Freeze the pie for 45 minutes until the syrup and ice cream hardens. Remove the pie from the freezer and spread the top with enough of the whipped topping to form a thin layer. Sprinkle the reserved peanut butter cup pieces on top of the pie. Freeze for about 1 hour before serving.

4

Cook on Low and Slow Down

ONE SUMMER VACATION while thawing out from a long New England winter, I realized I left my watch at home. "Of all things to forget, not my watch," I thought. I needed my watch, because on vacation we have schedules and appointments to keep, right? It took only about an hour to realize maybe the forgotten watch was a blessing. Three years later, I still have not put my watch back on.

For those of you like me who can be too structured, not wearing a watch has been liberating. Not having a watch attached to my wrist caused me to be a little more relaxed. Now, I'm not suggesting we completely ignore the structure of time; I'm simply making the point that racing against the clock isn't a healthy way to live. We all need to find our own pattern of simplicity because being in a hurry can create unwanted stress and anxiety, which could lead to unwanted health problems. Learning to slow down is possible, but it takes practice and patience.

My life was out of balance, working too much and resting too little. I began to notice how rushed my life was from trying to accomplish too much. Perhaps you, too, need to treat yourself to a time-out, a break, maybe even a midday siesta. Resting is a lost art in many modern, Western societies. Some cultures still cease from work in the middle of the day to refresh themselves with food and rest, and then go back to work. Our society would never allow such a practice, but there is wisdom in taking care of ourselves, body and mind. You are worth taking care of.

There are seasons and times when we need to finish tasks and complete projects, but after the goal is met, we need to rest. Remember the story of Creation, in which God created the Earth in six days and then rested on the seventh day. He took one-seventh of His week off, and He rested. If God deemed rest important, then so should we. According to the dictionary the word *rest* means "a state of refreshing after exertion," "to regain energy by means of relaxation," and "freedom from mental or emotional anxiety."[1] Do you need to regain energy or free yourself from mental or emotional stress? Jesus admonishes us in Matthew 11:28, "Come to Me, all you who labor and are heavy laden, and I will give you rest."

It's time to slow down and renew your mind and spirit. Allow yourself to be recharged and refreshed! And by the way, you don't have to feel guilty when you treat yourself to some rest and relaxation. You will be a better person—and probably a little nicer—when you allow yourself to rest.

 One Christmas a good friend of mine brought over peanut butter balls. I tried them, and they were chocolate-peanut butter bliss. The following recipe is from my friend, Verna Lilley. For all of you who are intimidated by the thought of making these delicious delights, this recipe is not difficult. It can also easily be cut in half to decrease the number of peanut butter balls it yields. Enjoy!

Peanut Butter Balls

Peanut butter mixture
   3 c. chunky peanut butter
   3 c. powdered sugar
   6 c. crisp rice cereal (such as Kellogg's Rice Krispies)
   ⅓ c. butter

Chocolate mixture
   3 12-oz. packages semi-sweet chocolate chips
   2 12-oz. packages milk chocolate chips

   Mix the ingredients for the peanut butter mixture together until combined. Butter your hands and roll the peanut butter mixture into small balls. Put the balls in the freezer for about 10 minutes. Meanwhile, melt the chocolate together in the microwave or over a double boiler. Take the peanut butter balls out of the freezer and begin to dip them into chocolate. Place the chocolate-covered peanut butter balls on a tray covered with wax paper. (If you used a microwave to melt the chocolate, work quickly during this stage so that the chocolate doesn't begin to harden before you can coat all the candies.) Let the balls stand about 10 minutes so that the chocolate hardens on the peanut butter balls. Store peanut butter balls in the refrigerator or a cool place.

   TIP In a pinch, I have used creamy peanut butter instead of chunky.

5

What Makes the Chocolate and Peanut Butter Valuable?

A LL YOU PEANUT butter cup lovers out there know the value of a peanut butter cup, but do you know that *you're* valuable? If you found a bag of peanut butter cups on your front porch, would you take the bag inside and eat them? Admit it. You would. You would say a quick prayer of thanks for the unexpected blessing, and then take the bag inside and eat them. How much more valuable are you than a bag of chocolate! Just like the peanut butter cup, you are not to be thrown away or disregarded.

Have you considered being thankful for the gift of your life? What about past triumphs and blessings that have brought you where you are today? Or perhaps trials have led you where you are. Regardless of your past, you are valuable and important.

In our culture, we often look at celebrities, politicians, and other public figures as being important and signifi-cant. We somehow esteem them higher than the ordinary person. We put people on a pedestal, looking at them as though they are flawless, without problems and pain, but when we look at ourselves we see our weakness and imper-fections. We conclude that we must be inferior and weak in comparison. Our value seems to be lessened in the light of others, but nothing could be farther from the truth. Many times we see the outward appearance of public figures and assume they have a perfect life because they *look* like they have it all together, but value is not based on finances or fame. Instead, it is based on the fact that God chose to create you.

You matter to God and to those around you. If God in His wisdom could help man to create the peanut butter cup, surely God can perfect you. You are not beyond repair, nor are you beyond His love and compassion. I encourage you to begin to see yourself as someone who matters, as someone who has something to offer to this world. Jeremiah 1:5 says, "Before I shaped you in the womb, I knew all about you. Before you saw the light of day, I had holy plans for you" (THE MESSAGE).

I am amazed at the good intentions that God has for each one of us. So the next time you're tempted to feel like you don't matter, STOP! Remember that you have been created on purpose. You are not an accident. Your life is valuable.

And by the way, don't forget to make time for an occasional good dessert.

This recipe is one I put together after many years of experimenting and taste-testing. This recipe went through many changes until I got it just right. This is a favorite of my kids, especially during the holidays. They frequently request this dessert for special occasions. I'm always happy to make it for them.

Chocolate-Peanut Butter Squares

Peanut butter mixture
1½ c. crushed graham crackers
1¼ c. peanut butter
1¾ c. powdered sugar
3 Tbsp. butter, melted

Chocolate mixture
3 Tbsp. shortening
16 oz. semi-sweet chocolate chips

Mix all the ingredients for the peanut butter mixture together and press into a 13 x 9-inch dish.

Melt the chocolate and shortening together in the microwave or over a double boiler. When completely melted, spread the chocolate over the pressed peanut butter mixture.

Refrigerate the pan until the chocolate gets firm (about 30 minutes).

6

Stop Stepping on the
Peanut Butter Cup

A RE YOU CRITICAL toward yourself? Do you ever berate
yourself for something you've said or done?

We are often harder on ourselves than anyone
else. We would not speak disrespectfully to our friends, yet at
times we verbally beat ourselves up. The idea is that we have
more respect for someone else than we do for ourselves. Do
you realize that we show someone respect because we value
them? If you are self-critical, the deeper question is, do you
value yourself? Do you respect yourself? Jesus said to love
your neighbor *as yourself.* (See Matthew 22:39.) How can we
love anyone else if we don't like who we are first?

It is a process to change your view of yourself, but it is
possible. I want to encourage you to quit putting yourself
down, and never let anyone else step on you. The older I get,
the more assertive I become. My neighbor once told me that
in her twenties she was a bit timid; in her thirties she got more
vocal; in her forties she began to stand up for herself; and
by the time she reached fifty, she discovered a boldness that
made her shine. You probably get the picture: you are worth
standing up for. However, the goal is for *you* to see *yourself* as
someone worth standing up for. The next time you're tempted
to put yourself down, don't.

Remember, you wouldn't step on a peanut butter cup because the peanut butter cup is worth respecting, and so are you!

There was a time when I was suffering with headaches. I had always heard that milk and dark chocolate can make a headache worse, so I decided to enter the world of white chocolate. Am I ever glad that I did! One evening, my family and I were watching a movie when I got a headache *and* a craving for a peanut butter cup. Out of desperation, I decided to make a simple peanut butter cup using white chocolate. My husband accidentally bought chunky peanut butter instead of smooth. I have never liked chunky peanut butter, but since that's all I had in my house, I decided to use it. This white chocolate-peanut butter cup was so delicious that everyone in my family loved it, except for one of my daughters, who will only eat the dark chocolate. That's okay, because this is one of the best peanut butter cups I have ever eaten!

White Chocolate-Peanut Butter Cups

12 oz. white chocolate chips
2 Tbsp. shortening
16 oz. chunky peanut butter (chunky peanut butter yields the best flavor)
24 large or 48 miniature cupcake liners

Melt the white chocolate with the shortening in the microwave or over a double boiler until the white chocolate is almost completely liquefied. Put the liners into a muffin or mini-muffin pan and spoon about 1 tablespoon white chocolate into the bottom of each liner. Spread the white chocolate up the sides of the liners and put the muffin pan into the freezer for 7 minutes or until the chocolate is hard. Pull the chocolate out of the freezer and spoon about 1–2 teaspoons of chunky peanut butter into each cup. Spread 1 tablespoon of the melted white chocolate on the top of the peanut butter layer in each cup. Refrigerate for about 30 minutes. Take out of refrigerator and serve.

Store in a cool place.

Tip You may substitute milk or dark chocolate chips for the white chocolate chips. I have done that to please both the dark and white chocolate lovers in my family!

7

The Refreshed Peanut Butter Cup

W E MUST MAKE time to allow ourselves to rest. Resting means "to cease activity," "to restore your energy by means of sleep," and to be in a state of "freedom from mental or emotional anxiety."[1] Doesn't that sound like a balanced life? The truth is, we all need to take a break from our routine activities, make sure we are getting enough rest, and let our minds rest from the cares of this world.

Have you ever found yourself feeling tired and grumpy? Perhaps you've felt exhaustion and been short with family members. Physical and mental fatigue has a way of creeping up on us and tempting us to lash out on others when we least expect it. Some of our weakness can be amplified when we're tired. For example, I find that I am more prone to worry when I am burnt out. My husband, who is usually very smart and analytical, cannot discuss serious issues with me when he's overly tired. We all have to recognize when our body sends us a signal to let us know its time to slow down, rest, and get some sleep. Dr. Don Colbert advocates sleep and laughter as important means of restoring health and boosting your body's immune response.[2]

Just recently I was discussing with someone whether vacations are a need or a want. I quickly made the case that vacations are a need. Now, the type of vacation someone takes could spill over into the want category, but the type of vacation I'm advocating is a break from your normal routine. This is a need. A simple vacation may mean an inexpensive camping trip or a one-day retreat. Find out what you can afford and go!

Just in case you need the affirmation to spend time on yourself, I'm encouraging you now. Yes, it's okay to take time out for yourself. You're not being selfish. The need to get refreshed is real. If God rested on the seventh day, we should follow His lead and do likewise.

Begin to find some time for rest. This may include something as simple as taking a nap. Personally, I find shopping relaxing. Maybe go get your nails done or read a good book. My husband likes to go for hikes in the mountains. Whatever you enjoy doing, make the time to unwind and relax. It is to your advantage (and everyone else's) that you take care of yourself and rest.

Take time out today and make a plan to find some relaxation.

This is the perfect recipe to go along with the idea of taking a break. It's delicious, and it's the easiest recipe in this book. This recipe was created during a time when I was fasting ice cream. I knew I couldn't eat ice cream, but I *could* find a way to put chocolate hard shell topping on peanut butter. This concoction yields the perfect chocolate-peanut butter taste without a lot of fuss, and as an added bonus, the rice cakes are good for you!

Chocolate-Peanut Butter Rice Cakes

4 rice cakes
4 Tbsp. peanut butter
1 bottle of chocolate hard-shell syrup (such as Hershey's Shell Topping)

Take each rice cake and spread 1 tablespoon of peanut butter on it. Put the rice cake in the freezer for 7 minutes. The rice cake should be cold. Drizzle the hard-shell chocolate syrup on it until you have covered the top of the rice cake and can no longer see the peanut butter. Put the chocolate-covered rice cake in the freezer for 10 more minutes. Take out of the freezer and eat immediately.

8

Creating Good Habits

D ID YOU KNOW that we feel what we think? In other words, if you're thinking discouraging, fearful thoughts, you're going to feel afraid and discouraged. If you're thinking angry and bitter thoughts, you're going to feel frustrated. The opposite is also true. If you're thinking energetic, encouraging thoughts, you will feel invigorated and inspired.

The good news is, negative thinking is just a bad habit that can be broken! Most of our behavior is learned from our surroundings and can be changed with time and patience. I came across a powerful excerpt from John Maxwell's book *Thinking for a Change* regarding the power of habits:

> *I am your constant companion. I am your greatest helper or heaviest burden. I will push you onward or drag you down to failure.*
>
> *I am completely at your command. Half of the things you do you might as well turn over to me and I will be able to do them quickly and correctly.*
>
> *I am easily managed—you must merely be firm with me. Show me exactly how you want something done and after a few lessons I will do it automatically.*

I am the servant of all great men; and alas, of all failures as well. Those who are great I have made great. Those who are failures, I have made failures.

I am not a machine, though I work with all the precision of a machine plus the intelligence of a man.

You may run me for profit or run me for ruin—it makes no difference to me.

Take me, train me, be firm with me, and I will place the world at your feet. Be easy with me and I will destroy you.

Who am I? I am a habit.[1]

Finally, a recipe that is good for you and still maintains the delicious combination of chocolate and peanut butter. The concept for this recipe started in a middle school health textbook. I came up with this combination after many attempts to create a healthier chocolate-peanut butter dessert. I think you will enjoy this!

Peanut Butter-Chocolate Granola

3 c. oatmeal, uncooked
¼ c. olive oil
⅔ c. honey
1 c. peanut butter
12 oz. semi-sweet chocolate chips

Preheat the oven to 325°. Mix the olive oil, honey, and peanut butter in a bowl. Add the oatmeal and stir the ingredients together. Spread in a 13 x 9-inch dish and bake for 15 minutes. Take the oatmeal mixture out of the oven and stir before patting the mixture back into place and putting the pan back in the oven for another 15 minutes. When it's ready, the mixture will be lightly browned. Spread the chocolate chips on top of the oatmeal immediately after taking the pan out of the oven.

Cool the granola before cutting it into squares. The final product can be stored in an airtight container for up to 5 days. If you prefer firmer granola, store it in the refrigerator.

9

Truth

ARE FEELINGS FACTS?
No. Feelings are not to be taken as facts. We filter our daily life through our own set of hurts and pain. I can't tell you the number of times my feelings have deceived me and almost ruined relationships.

I remember recently I was at work when a good friend of mine stopped by. She came and went without saying anything to me. I was devastated. I thought, "How could she not even say good-bye to me?" I later found out she had a family emergency that she had to attend to. If I would have based our relationship on my initial feelings, I would have been angry and disappointed in her. The truth was, something important came up with her family and she had to leave. I could have taken my hurt feelings and put a wall up in our relationship, but instead I recognized the truth and abandoned any wrong perceptions.

Our feelings can deceive us into focusing on the negative. There are times when we *feel* alone, but we are never truly alone. There are times when we *feel* afraid, but God says to fear not. There are times when we *feel* hopeless, but there is always a way out of a problem. Just because we feel a certain way, it does not mean our feelings are right. What do we focus our attention on? Where do we turn for truth? Truth can be found in the Scriptures. The Bible is an instruction manual for life. It speaks truths of comfort to our minds and peace to our heart.

It's very normal in our human experience to have times where we feel low, but the key is not to stay low. Sometimes life tries to knock the wind out of our sails, but we get back on board and keep sailing. Wherever you find yourself in life, don't quit and don't give up. God has promised that He would be a refuge for us. In fact, He has promised us that He "is able to do exceeding abundantly above all that we ask or think, according to the power that works in us" (Eph. 3:20). This assures us that God can do the impossible in our lives. He is able to go beyond what we could ask or think. Trust in God's promises for you.

You may want to take some time and locate scriptures that apply to your life. Put those scriptures where you will often read them. They will help keep your mind focused in the right direction. This is an important key when learning to stay positive and encouraged.

This recipe came out of a desire to eat Nutella with ice cream. I found it is incredibly delicious when the chocolate-hazelnut spread freezes at the bottom of a chocolate piecrust. I then figured out that cookies 'n cream ice cream complimented the flavors of the other ingredients very well. This experiment turned into a favorite that has received many compliments. And by the way, this pie takes under ten minutes to make!

Nutella Ice Cream Pie

1 pre-baked chocolate piecrust (such as Keebler Ready-Crust)
3½ c. cookies 'n cream ice cream
¼ c. of chocolate-hazelnut spread (such as Nutella), plus enough to drizzle on the top of the pie, about 3 Tbsp.
8 oz. whipped topping

Melt ¼ cup of the chocolate-hazelnut spread until soft enough to coat the bottom of the chocolate piecrust. Next, fill the pie shell with the ice cream, remembering to leave enough room for the whipped topping layer. Spread the desired amount of whipped topping on the pie, being sure to cover the ice cream completely. (If you find that the ice cream is too soft as you are adding the topping layer, put the pie in the freezer for 30 minutes to harden the ice cream. That will make it easier to add the next layer.) Melt the remaining 3 tablespoons of chocolate-hazelnut spread and drizzle over the top of the pie.

10

When the Chocolate Melts:
Dealing With Disappointment

AVE YOU EVER had chocolate melt in your hands? Has the heat on a summer day ever prevented you from handling and eating perfectly good chocolate? Just like heat can ruin perfectly good chocolate, so the trials of life can ruin our plans and dreams.

Out of all the different emotions that I've had to deal with, disappointment is by far the most challenging. Life's disappointments can turn into bitterness and resentment, *if* we choose to let it. During times when I have felt disappointment, I have made a decision to look, even search out, the good in a situation. I have learned there is always light at the end of the tunnel, even amidst disappointing circumstances.

Disappointment is defined in Webster's dictionary as, "defeated of; expectation, hope, desire, or design."[1] It takes much patience and perseverance to look beyond disappointment to determine to keep moving forward. The good news is that we don't have to let disappointment imprison us. In fact, a disappointment could be a blessing in disguise.

Disappointment can serve as a courage builder, a catalyst to mature us. For example, some time ago I was offered a job that I had always wanted. As it turned out, the job offer fell through, and I did not end up with the job. Initially, I was devastated. About six months later, I realized that job would have been the wrong path for me. Looking back, I became thankful that the job did not work out. I discovered that what we perceive to be disappointments can actually preserve us from moving in a wrong direction.

The opposite of disappointment is contentment. According to Webster's dictionary, *contentment* is "a resting, or satisfaction of mind."[2] Can you imagine being at rest in difficult circumstances? Contentment even in the midst of difficulties is possible when we let God do what only He can do, and then we rest in His very capable hands. This is when we find our peace and contentment.

Don't let disappointment leave you discouraged. Take courage and know that life's disappointments can bring positive change!

Who doesn't like chocolate cake with chocolate mousse? In this recipe, it's chocolate-hazelnut mousse that's getting paired with cake. This recipe is a keeper!

Chocolate-Hazelnut Mousse Cake

1 box chocolate cake mix
6 Tbsp. Nutella or other chocolate-hazelnut spread
8 oz. whipped topping
2 Tbsp. chocolate syrup
2 Tbsp. sour cream

Make the chocolate cake in a 13 x 9-inch pan according to package directions. When the cake is finished baking, set aside to cool.

First, fold the Nutella into the whipped topping. Then add the chocolate syrup and sour cream. Gently fold all ingredients together until creamy and smooth.

When the cake is completely cool, spread the mousse on top of the cake. Refrigerate for at least one hour before serving.

11

The Rejected Chocolate

W HEN OTHERS DON'T choose us, we often think to ourselves, "I've been rejected; I was not picked, chosen, or favored." We look inward as though there were a red X on our forehead. This sends a message that says, "I must not be worthwhile. Something is terribly wrong with me." The truth is, although we're not perfect, we are not internally flawed. All of us, at one point in our lives, have felt rejected.

I was just talking to a friend the other day who was magnifying her weakness. I quickly reminded her of all her strengths. The tone in her voice began to change, and she started to see her own value. She needed a little reminding that, though she felt rejected in one area of her life, she was not hopeless.

We need to be our own encourager. Remember to remind yourself that you are set apart and cherished greatly. You are made beautifully. God's works are marvelous, and you are His work. Picture God as the designer of a building and you as the building He is constructing. He took much time and put great thought into the structure and formation of His work. When He finished creating you, He looked at you and declared that His work was good. He is very proud of His work, and He takes delight in you because of it.

When someone rejects you for who you are, they are

rejecting God's blueprint. Stand strong and know that you are designed with greatness and purpose on the inside of you. Your worth does not diminish because someone rejects you.

 This pie is like silk. This recipe, like many of my recipes, came out of experimenting with something different to bring to a friend's house. Most of the time I experiment with whatever I have available in the refrigerator. In this case, the pie turned out to be one of my favorite chocolate cream pie recipes. This recipe is very simple and takes only about ten minutes to prepare.

Chocolate-Nutella Cream Pie

1 pre-baked chocolate piecrust (such as Keebler Ready-Crust brand)
½ of a 13 oz. jar of Nutella or other chocolate-hazelnut spread
8 oz. whipped topping
4 oz. cream cheese, softened
2 Tbsp. chocolate syrup
1 Tbsp. vanilla

Fold the chocolate-hazelnut spread into the whipped topping. Add the softened cream cheese, vanilla, and chocolate syrup and pour into the chocolate piecrust. Refrigerate for 3 hours or until firm before serving.

12

Your Future Will Be Better
Than Your Past

WHEN SOMEONE KNOWS they are loved and valued, they feel confident and can do anything, accomplish any goal. The opposite is also true. When someone feels they are unloved and lacks confidence, they accomplish very little. No matter what your past has been, know that you can make the decision to change the direction of your life.

If we're always recreating the past, how can we ever expect to move forward? If we're always dwelling on our mistakes, how can we ever expect to be successful? We have too much living to do, and we can't afford to waste any more time in the past. Better days are ahead. Everyone has to let go of regrets, bitterness, or past failures. If you don't, you will stay stuck! And who wants stagnation? We have to end the playback in our minds of past conversations, arguments, and entanglements. I recently heard someone say, it's all about our attitude. Our viewpoint on circumstances can work for us or against us. We get to decide.

I am currently reading a book called *What to Say When Talking to Yourself* by Shad Helmstetter, PhD. In his book, the author says that your brain is like a computer. Similar to a computer, what you program your mind to do and think is what your mind will do and think.[1] The book of Proverbs echoes a similar concept: "As [a man] thinks in his heart, so is he" (Prov. 23:7). We all need to recognize the power of our thoughts. The key is to reprogram your thoughts. You might ask how this is accomplished. It is done by replacing the old, negative thinking with new, uplifting, and encouraging thoughts.

Every new day we have the gift of the present moment to enjoy. We have the opportunity to explore new blessings, discover new beginnings. The book of Job in the Bible provides a great example of someone whose past gave way to a brighter future. The writer of Job tells us, "The LORD blessed the latter days of Job more than his beginning" (Job 42:12). Hang in there. If you refuse to give up, you will see victory over circumstances, and you will see your tomorrows turn into triumph.

What makes someone sure that his or her future will be successful? Endurance. It is his or her ability to stand in the midst of discouragement and adversity and wait until the hard circumstance passes. You know that our difficulties do pass. I think of Thomas Edison and his tireless efforts to develop the telephone. He was ridiculed for his determination, but he never gave up. He was criticized for his creativity, but he never quit. His endurance left an indelible mark in world history. Just like Edison, if you don't give up, your future will be better than your past. And who knows—perhaps you, too, will leave an indelible mark in history!

Many years ago I was traveling in Germany and had the opportunity to eat tiramisu in my cousin's Italian restaurant. I spent the next fifteen years trying to find a recipe that tasted just like the one I had in Germany. After many failed attempts of trying to find a good tiramisu recipe, I decided to create my own. The following recipe is so good it reminds me of the tiramisu I discovered those many years ago. I decided to name this dessert Restaurant Tiramisu because it tastes like the recipe from the restaurant in Germany.

Restaurant Tiramisu

Mascarpone mixture
3 8-oz. cartons of mascarpone cheese (often available in the specialty cheese section of your grocery)
8 oz. of whipped topping
½ c. of cooled coffee
2 Tbsp. of vanilla
1 c. of powdered sugar

Ladyfinger layer
8 c. of cooled coffee
4 Tbsp. chocolate syrup, divided
2 packages of ladyfingers (about 48 cookies)

Topping
2 Tbsp. cocoa
2 Tbsp. of powdered sugar

(continued on next page)

Mix mascarpone cheese, whipped topping, ½ cup of cooled coffee, vanilla, and powdered sugar in a mixing bowl for about 3 minutes or until all is well blended. Set aside.

Dip each ladyfinger into the bowl of coffee and immediately place them in the bottom of a 13 x 9-inch baking dish, making a layer of ladyfingers. Drizzle 2 tablespoons of chocolate syrup over the ladyfingers. Spread half of the mascarpone cheese mixture on top of the first layer of ladyfingers. (Tip: Rather than put the cheese in one lump over the soaked cookies before spreading, try distributing large spoonfuls of the cheese at regular intervals over the whole pan of ladyfingers. It will spread easier and will help maintain the integrity of the cookies underneath.)

Next, put another layer of coffee-dipped ladyfingers on top of the cheese. Drizzle the remaining 2 tablespoons of chocolate syrup over the second layer of ladyfingers, then add the remaining mascarpone mixture on top.

Combine the cocoa and remaining powdered sugar. Sift evenly on top of the dessert. Refrigerate at least one hour before serving. Keep refrigerated.

13

Breaking Barriers

W HAT BARRIER IS blocking you from fulfilling your purpose? What wall needs to be torn down in order for you to discover your gifts and talents? Sometimes we need to break the barriers of anger, unforgiveness, negativity, or (*fill in your wall here*) before we can move forward. It is time to break those barriers that block you from blossoming. It is time for you to move on.

You may be asking how. How can I get past these stumbling blocks? I have found two tactics that have been extremely helpful. The first one is to admit that there is a problem. Confront the problem. You may even have to seek out the help of a counselor or a good friend. The second helpful step is to bring any baggage or wrong thinking to God. Imagine bringing all your anger, unforgiveness, worry, etc. to the altar and leaving it there. If these same problems try to arise again, you may have to bring them back to the altar again and again. Don't let that baggage weigh you down. Yes, getting past the past can be a process that takes time. But it can be done, and the end result is worth the struggle. Make the decision to begin the process, realizing that change is possible.

There are many people who have gone before us and made positive changes in their lives. One person I admire is Paula Deen. She is one of the famous hosts on the Food Network. In her autobiography, *Paula Deen: It Ain't All About the Cookin'*, she tells of the many risks she took and the many positive strides she made in order to create a better life for herself.[1] She broke through her limiting barriers, and so can you.

The traits that you were born with are meant to impact your surroundings and maybe even the world. You were born with specific gifts and talents that are unique to you. There will never be anyone just like you. Begin to speak to the walls and barriers in your path and tell them to come down! Watch those walls fall. On the other side of your walls is freedom!

This recipe came out of my love for white chocolate and strawberries and cream. If you are a fan of fresh strawberries, you will love this cake. It's great for taking to parties or other gatherings.

White Chocolate-Strawberry Cake

1 box white cake mix
12 oz. of white chocolate, melted
2 c. of sliced strawberries, divided
8 oz. whipped topping
¼ c. of strawberry preserves or jelly

Bake the cake in two 9-inch cake pans according to the directions on the box, being careful not to overbake the cake. When the cake has cooled, put one of the layers on a cake plate and spread with the strawberry preserves.

Drizzle the melted white chocolate on top of the preserves according to your liking. I like to add enough that the top of cake is almost covered in white chocolate.

Spread 1½ cups of the sliced, fresh strawberries on top of the white chocolate. Spread half of the whipped topping over the strawberries.

Put the second cake on top of the whipped topping layer. Cover the top of the second cake with whipped topping and layer the remaining ½ cup of strawberries on top.

If desired, drizzle more white chocolate over the top of the cake.

14

God Delights in You

J UST LIKE THE peanut butter cup, you are a delight, but
you may be thinking, "How can God delight in me,
with all my faults?" The first thing you should know
is that everyone has made mistakes. The reality is that your
worth is not based on your behavior. God desires to show
you His kindness simply because you are His. We all want
someone to find us interesting and lovable. Children have
a need for their parents to show them unconditional love,
and adults need relationships that validate them. Do you ever
notice you feel your best around people who lift you up and
believe in you? Seek out people who encourage you. Begin to
limit your time with those who drag you down.

God believes in you, and He has good plans for you. He says
in His Word, "For I know the thoughts that I think toward
you, says the LORD, thoughts of peace and not of evil, to give
you a future and a hope" (Jer. 29:11). He has good plans for
you. As you turn to Him He will reveal His character to you,
and you will be encouraged to know how much He loves you.

God longs to rescue you from your enemies, from those
situations that appear to be impossible. In the book of Psalms,
David says, "[God] delivered me because He delighted in me"
(Ps. 18:19). It is similar to a parent rescuing their child out of
danger. If your child were drowning, you would not stop and

evaluate how good or bad that child had been. No! You would instinctively rescue him or her. God is the same way. He throws us a lifeline when the waves of life are attempting to drown us. He rescues us when we cannot rescue ourselves.

The next time you find yourself discontent and discouraged, remember that God delights in you. He did not create you to live in despair. Instead, He created you to live in joy and in peace. These promises are available for us. All we have to do is turn to Him.

 Chocolate and cream cheese are often a great combination. This recipe was another experiment that worked—and worked well! The key to this recipe is that the chocolate and cream cheese flavors are kept separated. If you are a fan of chocolate and a fan of cream cheese, you will love this dessert.

Chocolate Cream Cheese Pie

Crust
> 3 c. chocolate cookie crumbs
> 8 Tbsp. (1 stick) of butter, melted

Chocolate cream cheese filling
> 2 3.4-oz. boxes of instant chocolate pudding, prepared
> 8 oz. whipped topping
> 8 oz. cream cheese
> 1 Tbsp. vanilla
> ¾ c. powdered sugar
> 1 1.5-oz. chocolate bar

Crust

Stir the melted butter into the cookie crumbs and spread the mixture into the bottom of a 9-inch springform pan. Allow the crust to harden in the refrigerator for fifteen minutes.

Filling

Prepare the chocolate pudding according to the directions on the box. When thickened, spread the pudding on top of the chocolate crust.

Mix the cream cheese, powdered sugar, and vanilla together until smooth. Gently fold in the whipped topping until fully combined.

Spread the cream cheese mixture over chocolate pudding. (In order to help ensure that the layers do not mix, place large spoonfuls of the cream cheese mixture every 2 inches or so on the pudding. Then gently spread each spoonful to form a uniform layer.)

Shave or chop the chocolate bar and use as a garnish on top of the pie.

15

The Critical Candy Bar

I HAVE HAD TO crawl out of the pit of "critical self-talk" many times. In case you're wondering what critical self-talk is, it's talking to yourself in a way that belittles or berates you as a person. Can you believe we do this to ourselves? Many times we don't even recognize it.

The definition of being critical is "tending to find fault with somebody or something."[1] Do you ever look at yourself and find fault or disapprove of yourself? I have, and this is a very slippery slope. This mind-set actually inhibits you from moving forward. Take, for example, a recently graduated college student. If that graduate is critical toward herself as she applies for a job, it can hinder her from landing a good position. Even as she goes on interviews, chances are she is going to come across as having a lack of confidence. Her demeanor will depict someone who is unsure of her abilities, insecure, and, possibly, inept. Now compare this to a recently graduated college student who is confident and sure of her individual gifts and talents. The more confident graduate will most likely get the job.

Learning to like yourselves despite your flaws is a great achievement. Being critical of yourself does not reap anything good. What I have learned to do is replace critical self-talk with more comforting dialogue.

I was just talking to someone who is very critical of herself.

At the end of our conversation, I gave her a homework assignment. I wanted her to look in a mirror daily and say, "I love myself." When I told her this, she broke down in tears. It was such a foreign concept to her. I reminded her that the Bible says to love others as we love ourselves. How can we love anyone else if we don't like who we are? I ask you the same question, do you like who you are? Or are you critical and disapproving of yourself?

The way we talk to ourselves will move us either into success or defeat. Have you ever tuned into what you're saying to yourself? The average person has two hundred negative thoughts a day.[2] Don't be discouraged if you find that the way you talk to yourself is critical or negative. It takes time to change the way we talk to ourselves. We need to be patient and practice affirming self-talk. I assure you that after reading this you will be more aware of how you're talking to yourself.

If you are talking to yourself in a way that makes you feel down or fearful, tune in to what you're saying and begin to change your inner vocabulary. Begin to say things that will motivate and uplift your soul. The book of James says that the tongue is small, but its power is equivalent to that of the helm of a ship (James 3:4). This means that what we say enormously affects the direction of our life, just like huge boats are controlled by a comparatively small rudder. I always tell people, don't curse yourself. Don't say things like, "I will never change," or "I will always be stuck in this difficulty." Instead, replace those statements with, "I can change," or "I made a mistake, but I will do better next time."

Begin to find the silver lining in your clouds—there is always a silver lining!

My mom used to make this fun cake when I was younger, especially at Easter time. I have carried this tradition on with my daughters. They always look forward to decorating the cake with the jellybeans and licorice, but it doesn't have to be Easter to make it. This is one of those recipes that are equally as fun to make with kids as they are to eat.

By the way, I have made many chocolate bunny cakes due to the chocolate lovers in my house. Just use chocolate cake mix and substitute chocolate frosting for the strawberry. You can also be creative and shape the cake into something else and still decorate it with your kids. Enjoy the family time that this recipe creates!

Bunny Cake

1 box of white cake mix
1 can of strawberry frosting
1 bag of jellybeans
1 bag of red licorice

Bake the cake in two 9-inch cake pans according to package directions. When the cake is cool, put both layers side-by-side, touching, on a large cookie sheet. Do not stack the layers. Cut one of the cakes in half, then separate the two halves slightly to look like bunny ears. (See the diagram on the following page.)

Frost both cakes. Use jellybeans to create the bunny's eyes and nose and the licorice to make the bunny's smile. Also use the licorice to make a straight line on the bunny's ears.

Bunny Cake Diagram

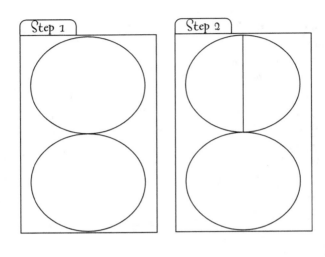

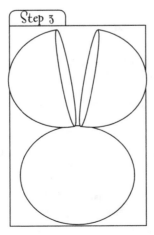

16

The Ideal Recipe

EVERYTHING YOU NEED to be successful in life is already in you. Yes, that's right. You have what it takes to accomplish any goal. God deposited the right amount of tenaciousness, intelligence, and skill into you. He gave you gifts and talents that will affect your world. Don't ever look at yourself as being inadequate; nothing is further from the truth. We all need guidance and direction, but with support, confidence, and the leading of the Holy Spirit, you can fulfill your aspirations.

Are you aware that there is no one like you? You are unique and valuable in your own right. What makes you important is the very fact that you were created; you have been born. Most of us base our significance on what we do and not on who we are. It is neither our accomplishments nor our lack of accomplishments that give us value. Rather, our value is based on who God says we are. The Bible teaches that He chose you simply because He loves you. In Psalm 139:13–17 God says:

> *For you formed my inward parts; You covered me in my mother's womb. I will praise You; for I am fearfully and wonderfully made; Marvellous are Your works, and that my soul knows very well. My frame was not hidden from You, When I was made in secret, And skillfully*

formed in the lowest parts of the earth. Your eyes saw my
substance, being yet unformed. And in Your book they
were all written, The days fashioned for me, when as
yet they were none of them. How precious also are Your
thoughts to me, O God! How great is the sum of them!

God knows exactly how He put you together. You are not a mistake or an accident. You have been meticulously designed. You are the ideal recipe!

I cannot say enough good things about this recipe. I have been making this for over a decade, and I have passed this recipe on many times through the years. You could almost put this dessert in the vegetable category. My kids' pediatrician once recommended a recipe like this to help me encourage my kids to eat vegetables, so you can feel good about enjoying the pumpkin flavor knowing it packs a healthier punch than other desserts.

Pumpkin Bread

½ c. of olive oil
2½ cups of granulated sugar
6 eggs
29 oz. of canned pumpkin
2 tsp. salt
3 tsp. cinnamon
3 tsp. vanilla
1½ tsp. baking powder
4⅔ cups of flour
3 tsp. baking soda, diluted in 1 c. of water

Preheat the oven to 350°. Mix all the ingredients together. Grease and flour three loaf pans and divide the batter between them. Bake for one hour or until knife inserted comes out clean. Cool before slicing.

17

Lost Your Flavor?

*H*AS LIFE EVER knocked the wind out of you? I have found myself flat on my back a few times. When this happens, I go on a quest to regain my peace. I will go back to God and pray and regroup. I will find something positive to focus on. There is always hope; there is always some ounce of strength left. I have developed the mind-set that refuses to stay down or look at the negative. I may fall, but I'm not staying down—and neither should you! Begin to remind yourself that there is always a bright side to focus on.

One of my favorite movies is *Rocky*.[1] The continual message throughout the movie is that Rocky will rise again. At the end of the movie, just when it looks like Rocky is going to loose, the music begins to change, along with his mental outlook. He begins to regain his strength. He looks beaten down and unable to win, but you see the determination on his face. There is a confidence to win in his eyes. He seems to be saying, "Come on; give me your best shot." He knows that he can win. On the other side of the screen, you're sitting on the edge of your seat going, "Rocky! Rocky!" Admit it; there is a part of you that has inwardly cheered him on. Rocky is the ultimate underdog because he keeps getting back up. He continues to make a comeback. I want you to see a little of yourself in Rocky Balboa.

Even though you've taken a beating by the storms of life, get back up! Change your mental outlook. Begin to see yourself through the eyes of God. Let your perspective change, and watch how disappointment begins to fade and encouragement begins to emerge. We were designed for victory, for freedom. We have spiritual and mental muscles that we didn't even know existed. It's time to start training for a new round, a new and better season of life.

Don't lose your flavor. Add some stamina and zeal into your life. You have what it takes to win. You have what it takes to be successful.

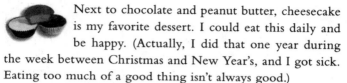 Next to chocolate and peanut butter, cheesecake is my favorite dessert. I could eat this daily and be happy. (Actually, I did that one year during the week between Christmas and New Year's, and I got sick. Eating too much of a good thing isn't always good.)

This recipe is so easy to make, and it will compete with any baked cheesecake recipe. This is good on a hot summer day or during the holidays.

Easy Cheesecake

3 8-oz. packages cream cheese, softened
¾ c. sugar
3 Tbsp. vanilla
8 oz. whipped topping
1 graham cracker crust
1 can strawberry or cherry pie filling

Mix the cream cheese and sugar until well blended. Add the vanilla and continue to blend. Fold in the whipped topping and spread the mixture into the piecrust. Refrigerate for at least two hours. Put the fruit topping on right before serving.

18

When the Baker Burns Out

*H*AVE YOU EVER hit rock bottom because of stress and fatigue? Have you ever experienced some kind of burnout from all the responsibilities you have? Sometimes we need a time-out!

Taking care of ourselves prevents burnout. This means allowing downtime and planning fun things to do. This means scheduling in something that we enjoy doing. Hobbies can be a good source of relaxation, but there are times when just listening to good music or being outdoors can be relaxing. It doesn't have to be expensive to be effective.

After you have had some time to get refreshed, you will have a better perspective on life. You will probably even be a nicer person. Have you ever found yourself being short with people when you're burnt out, especially with those you love? That's a signal it's time to let yourself be free from the daily grind.

I have found exercise to be a great way to relax. There is something about the body in motion that releases a sensation of strength and vigor. Taking a walk or jogging can help the body and mind to decompress. Exercise can be equated to letting off steam, and in today's busy world, we sure need that. Unfortunately, more people do not take advantage of this stress release.

I remember one spring I experienced intense stress due to difficult circumstances in my life. I felt so much emotional strain that I felt I was going to snap. I needed a vacation. I needed time out from my routine. What my family and I did was to jump on a plane and head south. I can still remember baking in the hot Georgia sun and letting all the stress and pressure just burn off.

Maybe getting on a plane and going far away isn't possible for your lifestyle, but you can do something. Take a vacation or go out to dinner—let someone else do the cooking; time to treat yourself to something good. You are worth a time-out so that you don't burn out. Whatever it's going to take to recharge your batteries, *do it*. Maybe you're not even sure anymore what fun means to you. Maybe you don't know how you would spend time relaxing. Spend some time writing down ways you like to relax then do some creative planning and schedule relaxation and leisure time into your life. It's time to take time out and make relaxing a priority. There is a new beginning waiting to bloom in your life.

By the way, don't forget to stop and enjoy a good dessert along the way!

If you're looking for an alternative to a chocolate dessert, this recipe from my mom will not disappoint. When I was kid, she would make this in the summertime. I remember enjoying the moist cake with fruit topping. For a kid to like a fruit dessert you know it had to be good!

Moist Jell-O Cake

1 box white cake mix
1 3-oz. package strawberry Jell-O
1 21-oz. can cherry or strawberry pie filling
8 oz. whipped topping
8 oz. white chocolate, melted

Prepare the cake in a 13 x 9-inch pan according to box directions. When the cake is done, let it cool for about 30 minutes.

While the cake is cooling, prepare the Jell-O according to package directions. Do not refrigerate the liquid.

Using a toothpick, poke lots of holes all over the cake. Pour the liquid Jell-O over the cake to saturate the cake, allowing it to sink into the toothpick holes. Drizzle the melted white chocolate over the top of the cake. Next, spread the cherry or strawberry pie filling over the cake, followed by the whipped topping.

Refrigerate for at least 2 hours to chill the topping and allow the Jell-O to become firm.

19

Who Said the Cocoa Bean Wouldn't Become Chocolate?

ONE OBSTACLE I have had to overcome is the naysayers in my life, people around me who said my dreams were impossible and ridiculous or who have said, "You're reaching too high; come back to reality." I've had people around me who said nothing, but gave me that look that let me know they disapproved of my goals. Negative looks are probably worse than negative words, because at least you can confront the words.

Who we associate with will either skyrocket us up to success or bring us down to defeat. It's important to have supportive people around you who aren't threatened by your goals and someone who will encourage you to succeed. We all need people who will cheer us on. In the same way, we need to search out people we can cheer on and motivate to reach their dreams. What you sow is what you will reap in this area. You know, it's like that old expression, If you need a friend, then be a friend.

Perhaps you've had ideas and dreams that God has placed in your heart, but you've wondered if any of it will ever come to pass. Let me encourage you: it's no accident you're reading this right now. You need to know that are created with purpose and potential. Stephen Covey said, "Begin with the end in mind."[1] Revisit your goals and write them down to come up with a vision statement, or a plan of action. If you have no goals in life, you will aimlessly wander through it. Lewis Carroll expressed this well when he wrote, "If you don't know where you are going, any road will get you there."[2] Successful people have goals; they have a direction, a path to follow. I want to encourage you to get excited about planning for your future. Have fun following your goals.

I was recently watching a very talented singer on TV. She testified that it took her twelve years of persistent faith to get a recording contract. This woman got up to sing and she sang beautifully. Just like this gifted singer, if it takes years for your dreams to come to fruition, don't give up!

 I have been perfecting this chocolate chip cookie recipe for many years. I use half the sugar of other recipes, and I use a combination of butter and olive oil. You still get the butter flavor, but the olive oil serves as a healthier ingredient that keeps the cookie moist. Trust me, you cannot tell the difference between this chocolate chip cookie and other, more fattening chocolate chip cookies.

The key to a good chocolate chip cookie is to be sure it's not overbaked. I always take the cookies out just before the timer says they're done to make sure they stay a little gooey. This chocolate chip cookie indulgence is almost too good to be true.

Chocolate Chip Cookies

½ c. (1 stick) butter, softened
½ c. olive oil
1 c. packed brown sugar
2 tsp. vanilla extract
1 tsp. salt
2 large eggs
2¼ c. all-purpose flour
1 tsp. baking soda
12 oz. chocolate chips

Preheat the oven to 375°. Mix the butter, olive oil, and sugar in a large bowl. Add vanilla, salt, and eggs before stirring in the flour and soda. After the batter is well blended, fold in the chocolate chips and stir a few times with a spoon. Drop the cookies on an ungreased cookie sheet and bake for 8 minutes or until light brown for gooey cookies. For firmer cookies, bake for 10 minutes.

TIP Many times I will use a mixture of 1¼ cups all-purpose flour and 1 cup rice flour. This reduces the amount of gluten in the cookies, which is a helpful adjustment for people with special dietary requirements.

20

The Tempting Dessert

OK, WHO HAS never felt the pull of temptation? We all have at some point. It doesn't matter if the temptation is a luring piece of chocolate cake when you've already had enough to eat or the desire to spend money you don't have. Whatever is pulling at you, you have the ability to withstand the temptation. When Jesus was tempted, He responded by quoting the Word of God to the temptation. (See Luke 4:1–13.) If this worked for Jesus, I know it will work for you and me.

We know deep in our soul when temptation is pulling us in a destructive direction. We're all tempted in different ways, but whatever your temptation is, listen to that alarm that goes off in your mind that says, "Wait! Proceed with caution; there's danger ahead." We were designed with a conscience to know the difference between right and wrong. We all need to be sensitive to that still, small voice that keeps us from danger. I have found it helpful to talk to someone I trust and tell them about a specific struggle. Oftentimes just exposing the struggle will deflate the temptation.

Sometimes we fall into that daydream mind-set. This mind-set tries to convince us that wrong is really right. Many times we know what is right for us, but for a moment, we struggle. I am a firm believer that hanging in there and doing the right thing will reap a good outcome.

So let's not allow ourselves to get fatigued doing good.
At the right time we will harvest a good crop if we don't
give up, or quit.

—Galatians 6:9, THE MESSAGE

Many times we are tempted to choose the wrong path because of unmet needs. Tune in to what you're really feeling when you're being tempted. Perhaps there are old wounds that you're trying to fill through that temptation. Other times temptation strikes because we live in a fallen world. Either way, be prudent and wise and avoid the temptation.

Choosing the right road will lead us to a pleasant outcome. Choosing the wrong road could lead us to devastating consequences. During times of temptations, we need to remind ourselves of the ill consequences that potentially await us. This makes the temptation less appealing.

Which road will you choose? Whether it's a second piece of chocolate cake or a more serious, life-altering decision, we need to think about the end result.

This dessert is incredibly refreshing and light. There are only four ingredients in this pie, and it can practically be made with your eyes closed. My mom has made this recipe for years, and it's one of my favorites. No one will ever know this pie took five minutes to put together.

Frozen Lime Pie

1 graham cracker crust
1 14-oz. can sweetened condensed milk
¾ c. frozen limeade concentrate (found in the freezer section of your grocery), softened slightly
4 oz. cream cheese
8 oz. whipped topping

Mix sweetened condensed milk with the limeade concentrate. Add cream cheese and mix well. Fold in whipped topping. Blend all ingredients together. Pour ingredients into piecrust. Freeze for at least 2 hours. Store in freezer.

21

The Dessert That Tries
to Be Perfect

FOR ALL YOU perfectionists out there, myself included, here's a reminder: perfection isn't possible. I realize I may have just burst your bubble, but this truth will set you free. There is only One that is perfect, and His name is spelled G-o-d.

The definition of *perfect* is "to be without errors, flaws, or faults."[1] I do not fit this definition, nor do I know anyone who does. Usually we see the outward appearance of others and presume they are close to perfection, but when you get close enough to those you deem perfect, you will find that everyone has flaws.

We all have weaknesses and imperfections. This is part of being human. Many times we put ourselves down as we're trying to work through our flaws. Imagine a parent who consistently berated their child as that child was earnestly trying to work through his or her shortcomings. After a while that child would feel like a failure and think that he could never change. Yet this is what we do to ourselves. This creates a mentality of defeat. We can offer forgiveness to others, but when it comes to ourselves we demonstrate very little mercy. It's time to change. Remember that your thinking is a habit, and it takes time and practice to change habits. The good news is that it can be done!

I have to go to God in prayer and depend on His strength to help me daily. The apostle Paul said this of God: "And He said to me, 'My grace is sufficient for you, for My strength is made perfect in weakness. Therefore most gladly I will rather boast in my infirmities, that the power of Christ may rest upon me" (2 Cor. 12:9). The apostle Paul is saying that it's in our weaknesses that God's strength rests on us. God comes along and empowers us. When we're weak, He is strong. When we're imperfect, He is perfect.

The desire to be perfect comes from a need to prove your worth. I have spent countless hours critiquing my every word and deed. I have a great motto now: I did the best I could, and that's good enough. Try saying that out loud. This motto takes a lot of unnecessary pressure off our shoulders.

Ask yourself, what am I truly responsible for? What can I delegate? What area of my life can I give up being perfect in? It's okay to let others see your imperfections. People would rather listen and learn from people who are able to share their struggles and weaknesses, because it teaches us how they overcame their struggles. How can we learn from someone who has never gone through difficulties? Jesus was perfect and sinless, but Hebrews 4:15 tells us that He was tempted in all ways, which makes Him well able to sympathize with us in our struggles. This gives us hope that we, too, can overcome our own difficulties.

The Bible compares God to a potter and us to clay. (See Isaiah 64:8.) We are each a work in progress. Let's do our best and leave the results to God!

This recipe came from my husband's grandmother, June Calvert. My mother-in-law gave me this delicious recipe. It's a nice change from the traditional pumpkin pie recipes that are circulating today. I also like the idea of using regular milk, as opposed to evaporated milk. If you have a love of pumpkin recipes, this one is a tried-and-tested winner!

Mother's Pumpkin Pie

1½ c. pumpkin
¾ c. of sugar
1 egg
1¼ c. milk
2 Tbsp. light corn syrup
1 Tbsp. cornstarch
½ tsp. salt
1 tsp. cinnamon
¼ tsp. ginger
¼ tsp. nutmeg
1 frozen piecrust, thawed

Preheat the oven to 425°. Combine the pumpkin and sugar. Add remaining ingredients and stir well. Pour into an unbaked pie shell and bake for ten minutes at 425°. Then turn the oven temperature down to 325° and bake for 35 to 40 minutes or until a knife inserted in the center comes out clean.

22

Facing Obstacles

W E ALL FACE obstacles in our lives, times when the odds seem stacked against us and we don't see any way out. During those struggles, we may seem to loose all courage and confidence that we can overcome our giants, but we must remember that our personal victories begin in our minds. The book of Proverbs says, "As [a man] thinks in his heart, so is he" (Prov. 23:7). If we think of ourselves as weak and ineffective, then we will be weak and ineffective. If we look at ourselves as strong and courageous, then we will be strong and courageous.

There are people in Scripture that saw themselves as having no strength. The Israelites saw themselves as grass-hoppers in comparison to their foes, a tribe of strong giants (Num. 13:33), and David described himself as a worm (Ps. 22:6). This is no way to go into battle. When you face the giants in your life, how do you see yourself? Do you question your ability to make it through hard times? Winning our battles hinges on knowing that God has equipped us with everything we'll ever need to win. When you have faith in the One who created all things, you have the beginning of your victory.

What's the difference between someone who wins and someone who loses? The difference is that the loser forgets that God is right there with him to help him face the battle.

I want you to get a picture of your heavenly Father standing right behind you. When your enemy faces you, he's also facing your heavenly Father. Many times we see our enemy in front of us, but we don't see or hear God behind us saying, "You have what it takes; I have enabled you and equipped you to fight *and* to win." Many times we are too afraid to even face our giants because we have no confidence in God or in ourselves. I have had to pick myself up a number of times and remind myself that God has designed me to win—and He has designed you to win!

The next time you're facing obstacles, remember you are not alone. The One who created everything is the One who is standing beside you.

 This recipe is one of my favorite pumpkin recipes. I came up with this because I absolutely love using vanilla cake mix as a dessert crust. I was sure I could find something to put in it. Of course, a pumpkin pie mixture was the perfect fit. And yes, this could also be topped with whipped cream or my personal favorite, vanilla ice cream.

Pumpkin Pie Squares

Crust
  1 box vanilla cake mix
  ½ c. (1 stick) butter
  1 egg

Pie filling
  2 15-oz. cans pumpkin
  3 eggs
  1 c. milk
  ⅔ c. packed brown sugar
  4 tsp. cinnamon
  ¼ tsp. nutmeg
  2 Tbsp. vanilla

Preheat the oven to 375°. Grease a 15 x 10-inch jelly roll pan or other 1-inch deep cookie sheet.

Using a fork, mix together the cake mix, egg, and softened butter in a small bowl. Blend the ingredients until the mixture resembles a dough, then press into the bottom of a greased cookie sheet to form a crust. (If the mixture seems too sticky to form a dough, add a tablespoon of flour at a time until the desired texture is reached.)

To make the filling, mix all of the ingredients together. Pour the mixture over the crust and bake for 35 minutes or until set.

23

Timing

W HEN WILL THINGS change? When will this difficulty end? When will this pain go away? The list
of questions we ask during stressful or hurtful
situations could go on and on.

We all get weary while waiting for change. We want answers
to tough questions. But when difficulties are out of our control,
we need to give our struggles over to God. In His timing,
circumstances will change. In His timing, we will be trans-
formed. In His timing, the tough questions will be answered.

I know what it's like to try to change yourself and your
circumstances in your own strength, to no avail. When we
are void of our own strength, we are then in a position to
look up for help. When our resources are exhausted, we are
then in a posture to seek God. When problems arise that I
cannot solve, I ask God for help. I ask Him to reveal a scripture to me that is applicable to what I'm going through.

I recall a time in my life when a problem arose that caused
me to seek God's perspective. I found a lump in my breast
that needed to be checked out, so I went to the doctor. He
sent me for a mammogram and ultrasound. After these tests,
I was sure the doctor would tell me the lump was nothing
to be concerned about. But that's not what happened. My
timing was very different from God's timing. Soon after the

mammogram and ultrasound, the doctor recommended that I see a breast surgeon. The very suggestion of seeing someone whose title is "breast surgeon" is unnerving, but I went. At that point I began to pray, fast, and ask God for a specific scripture that would apply to my situation. God was faithful. He revealed a scripture that spoke directly to my situation, and I began to quote this scripture over and over until it became a truth to me.

> *No evil shall befall you, Nor shall any plague come near your dwelling.*
>
> —Psalm 91:10

I believed that no plague or (disease) would come upon me. So off I went to the breast surgeon. The doctor preformed one minor biopsy, and I was sure the results would come back favorable. The results came back, but they were not favorable. There was a concern over one of the cell tissues and the doctor felt it was necessary to do a second, more serious biopsy. Of course I was scared, but I kept reminding God that He had given me a promise that "no plague would come near my dwelling." I didn't understand why all that was happening, but I made the decision to trust the promise God gave me. Before long, the results from the second biopsy came back. This time, the results *were* favorable. I finally got a clean bill of health. Why God allowed all those tests and trips to the doctors, I don't know; but I do know that in God's timing the end result was good.

While it's true that we need to take action and do everything that we can and should do to get through difficulties, we also need to stand and wait for God's timing. The apostle Paul said, "And having done all...stand. Stand therefore, having girded your waist with truth" (Eph. 6:13–14). When I was waiting to get those test results back, I was standing. Hope and faith in the truth of God's Word and His promises were continually at my side. When you are facing a crisis, do what you know to do and then stand firm in the knowledge that God is taking care of the rest. This is the kind of faith that looks hopelessness in the eye and defies its impossibilities.

Our personal timetable is different from God's timetable. He's never early or late, but always right on time. It is our faith in His promises that keeps us from sinking. With our faith and His timing, we can overcome life's obstacles. We can be certain that God will not give us more than we can handle.

 This recipe is from my mother-in-law, Ann. I remember she made these when my husband and I were first married, and I fell in love with them. The scent of baking apples will make you want to curl up on the couch and watch a good movie. This is a great recipe to make when it's cold outside and you want to snack on something warm. Not to mention, you get all the benefits and nutrients of the apples.

Apple Dumplings

Apple syrup
   ¾ c. sugar
   ⅓ c. butter
   1⅓ c. hot water
   Dash of cinnamon and nutmeg
(continued on next page)

Combine the above ingredients over medium heat. Stir until sugar is dissolved.

Dumpling

1 15-oz box of piecrust (such as Pillsbury brand piecrusts in the refrigerator section, which come rolled up)

4 large apples, diced

1 tsp. cinnamon

¼ tsp. nutmeg

sugar to taste

¼ tsp. salt

1 Tbsp. flour

Preheat the oven to 425°.

Toss the diced apples, cinnamon, nutmeg, sugar, salt, and flour in a bowl until the apples are evenly coated.

Cut out six 7-inch squares from the piecrust dough. Place 2 tablespoons of the apple mixture in the center of each square of dough. Fold the edges of dough up around the apples in the center of the dumplings. Seal the top by wetting the edges of the dough slightly and gently pressing together.

Place the dumplings in a 13 x 9-inch baking dish. Pour the prepared syrup over each apple dumpling. Bake at 425° for 10 minutes, then reduce the heat to 350° and bake for another 25 to 30 minutes or until the crust browns. Top with vanilla ice cream or whipped cream.

24

The Determined Baker

W HERE ARE YOU right now in your life? Are you satisfied with your job? What about your mission in life? Are you accomplishing your dreams and goals, or have you settled for a mediocre life? Would you be quick to tell me the reasons why you were unable to finish what you set out to do? Have you lost your determination? If you have, it's time to get it back. It's time to refocus and determine to once again go after your dreams.

Recently I was watching *Rudy*, a movie that tells the real story of a young man who was extremely determined to reach his goal of playing football for the University of Notre Dame. The problem was, he was shorter than most players, not very good in school, and his family lacked the finances to send him. In the midst of fighting to overcome these obstacles, his father sat him down and told him he wasn't smart enough or athletic enough to play football. The rest of the movie chronicles his plight to overcome his weaknesses and accomplish his dream of playing football for Notre Dame.

By the end of the movie tears were rolling down my face as Rudy accomplished his dream. Even his father watches in disbelief as Rudy achieves his goal. He had everything working against him, but what he had working for him was his faith and his determination. If he could overcome his obstacles with all his limitations, so can you.

Is there something in your life that you would like to achieve? Like Rudy, have you been told you don't have what it takes? On the contrary, you do have the stamina and persistence to reach your objectives. The truth is, you are created with purpose and potential. You can achieve your goals. God has put giftings and ambitions on the inside of you, but only you can make the decision to cooperate with Him to fulfill your destiny.

Determination, the refusal to surrender in the midst of adversity, is what makes someone a success. Another word for *determination* is "resolve." To be determined means to have a fixed purpose. When you're determined, nothing can stop you. When you are determined, you are steadfast, immovable.

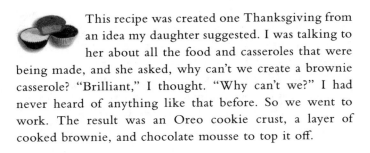 This recipe was created one Thanksgiving from an idea my daughter suggested. I was talking to her about all the food and casseroles that were being made, and she asked, why can't we create a brownie casserole? "Brilliant," I thought. "Why can't we?" I had never heard of anything like that before. So we went to work. The result was an Oreo cookie crust, a layer of cooked brownie, and chocolate mousse to top it off.

Oreo Brownie Casserole

3 c. Oreo cookie crumbs (you can buy them crumbled or put some Oreos into a food processor to chop them up)
½ c. (1 stick) butter, melted
1 box brownie mix
2 3.4-oz. boxes instant chocolate pudding
8 oz. whipped topping
2 tsp. vanilla
⅛ tsp. almond extract (optional)

Prepare the brownie mix according to package directions. Set them aside and allow them to cool.

Meanwhile, mix the melted butter into the crushed Oreo cookies. Press the mixture into the bottom of a 13 x 9-inch baking dish. Put the pan in the refrigerator to chill while finishing the rest of the recipe.

Make the pudding according to the box directions for pie filling. When the pudding has set completely, gently fold in the whipped topping, vanilla, and almond extract.

Take the Oreo crust out of refrigerator. Crumble the cooked brownies over the crust layer. Next, spread the pudding mixture over the brownies. Chill the layered casserole for at least 2 hours.

Conclusion

WHEN I THINK of life, I think of freedom—freedom to choose optimism, freedom to choose confidence, freedom to choose God. Even on gloomy days we have the freedom to let sunshine rule in our hearts. When stress tries to envelope us, we have the freedom to seek a reprieve. We have the choice to focus on what is right in our life instead of what is wrong. We have the freedom to see our situations from a position of strength rather than a position of weakness. Will we magnify the blessings in our lives or will we magnify the adversities that attempt to defeat us?

I remember one January when my husband went on a business trip to Holland. The day he left was cloudy and gray with snow falling from the sky. That afternoon after he left, I fed the kids, and then I went and sat down with a piece of Oreo brownie casserole (honestly I did). I looked out the window and I made the decision that I was going to, on purpose, enjoy my week. I resolved that this was going to be a great week. I was going to find the blessing and gift of each new day. I was determined to learn and laugh from each new experience. I had a great week. The choice was mine, and I chose to search out silver linings.

We can sum our life up in three areas: our relationship to our Creator, our relationship to our family members, and our purpose on this Earth. Ask yourself, do you have a relationship with God? Have you told your loved ones how much you love and appreciate them? Do you communicate to those who are important to you? And lastly, have you discerned your purpose on this Earth? What is it that you enjoy doing? If you could roll out of bed with no obligations, how would you spend your day? What is your purpose?

There have been times I have come to the conclusion that my life is full and satisfying. Is everything perfect? Of course not, but the things that matter most to me are in alignment. How about you? What areas in your life would you like to adjust? I encourage you to sit down with a favorite piece of dessert—yes, I said your favorite dessert—and plan a new road map for your future.

If you seek fulfillment from the three categories listed above, you will not come up empty. Your life will be content and productive. Will you be free from the trials and storms of life? No, but you when you have strong foundations in your life, peace is attainable.

All things are possible for your future. A good life begins between your ears. A wise statesman once said:

> *Nothing can stop the man with the right mental attitude from achieving his goal; nothing on earth can help the man with the wrong mental attitude.*[1]
>
> —THOMAS JEFFERSON

It's up to you to awake and dream. The time for change is now.

Notes

Chapter 2
The Faithful Baker

1. Hebrew definition found at http://www
.searchgodsword.org/lex/heb/view.cgi?number=02388
(accessed January 8, 2008).

Chapter 3
Don't Condemn the Chocolate

1. *Noah Webster's Dictionary 1828 Edition Facsimile*
(Chesapeake, VA: Foundation for American Christian
Education, 2000), s.v. "condemnation."

2. Rick Meyers, *e-Sword* (http://www.e-sword.net/
index.html), s.v. "Romans 8:1."

Chapter 4
Cook on Low and Slow Down

1. *MSN Encarta Dictionary,* s.v. "rest," http://encarta
.msn.com/dictionary_/rest.html (accessed January 7,
2008).

Chapter 7
The Refreshed Peanut Butter Cup

1. *MSN Encarta Dictionary,* s.v. "rest," http://encarta
.msn.com/dictionary_/rest.html (accessed January 8,
2008).

2. Don Colbert, MD, *The Seven Pillars of Health* (Lake Mary, FL: Siloam, 2007).

Chapter 8
Creating Good Habits

1. John C. Maxwell, *Thinking for a Change: 11 Ways Highly Successful People Approach Life and Work* (New York, NY: Warner Faith, 2008), 12.

Chapter 10
When the Chocolate Melts— Dealing With Disappointment

1. *Webster's Dictionary*, s.v. "disappointment."

2. Ibid., s.v. "contentment."

Chapter 12
Your Future Will Be Better Than Your Past

1. Shad Helmstetter, *What to Say When You Talk to Yourself* (New York, NY: Pocket Books, 1990).

Chapter 13
Breaking Barriers

1. Paula Deen and Sherry Suib Cohen, *Paula Deen: It Ain't All About the Cookin'* (New York, NY: Simon and Schuster, 2007), 36.

Chapter 15
The Critical Candy Bar

1. *MSN Encarta Dictionary,* s.v. "critical," http://encarta.msn.com/dictionary_/critical.html (accessed January 7, 2008).

2. "Self Talk," from audiotape series *Attacking Anxiety and Depression,* distributed by The Midwest Center for Stress and Anxiety (1998).

Chapter 17
Lost Your Flavor

1. *Rocky,* directed by John G. Avildsen (Chartoff-Winkler Productions, 1976).

Chapter 19
Who Said the Cocoa Bean
Wouldn't Become Chocolate?

1. "Quotes for Goals," Motivatingquotes.com, http://motivatingquotes.com/goalsq.htm (accessed January 7, 2008).

2. "Lewis Carroll," Thinkexist.com, http://thinkexist.com/quotes/lewis_carroll/ (accessed January 7, 2008).

Chapter 21
The Dessert Who Tries
to Be Perfect

1. *MSN Encarta Dictionary,* s.v. "perfect," http://encarta.msn.com/dictionary_/perfect.html (accessed January 7, 2008).

Conclusion

1. "Quotes for Goals," Motivatingquotes.com, http://www.motivatingquotes.com/goalsq.htm (accessed March 13, 2008).

Recipe Index

Chocolate-Peanut Butter Desserts

Cookies and Cakes

Nutella Desserts

Pies

Pumpkin Desserts

Favorite Miscellaneous

Other Books by This Author

THE TIMELESS TREASURE: A COMMENTARY ON THE SONG OF SOLOMON

This book is a great Bible study guide to understanding the Song of Solomon. *The Timeless Treasure* is a must for anyone who wrestles with doubting their own worth and value.

10-digit ISBN: 0-9746602-0-5

13-digit ISBN: 978-0-9746602-0-2

AN ENCOURAGING WORD

God is never blindsided by what is going on in your life. He has a plan for you, and He is never out of control. The bad times are only temporary. *An Encouraging Word* unearths scriptural truths that will edify anyone who is exhausted and fears that things may never get better.

10-digit ISBN: 1-59185-715-5

13-digit ISBN: 978-1-59185-715-0

To Contact the Author

To contact Luann Dunnuck or to have her speak at
your organization's meeting please inquire at:

GSTreasure@aol.com

(203) 770-1074